Celebrate Cinco de Mayo

Other titles in the *Celebrate Holidays* series

Celebrate Chinese New Year
ISBN 0-7660-2577-2

◆

Celebrate Cinco de Mayo
ISBN 0-7660-2579-9

◆

Celebrate Columbus Day
ISBN 0-7660-2580-2

◆

Celebrate Halloween
ISBN 0-7660-2491-1

◆

Celebrate Martin Luther King, Jr., Day
ISBN 0-7660-2492-X

◆

Celebrate St. Patrick's Day
ISBN 0-7660-2581-0

◆

Celebrate Thanksgiving Day
ISBN 0-7660-2578-0

Celebrate Cinco de Mayo

Joanne Mattern

These women dance during a Cinco de Mayo celebration.

Enslow Publishers, Inc.
40 Industrial Road
Box 398
Berkeley Heights, NJ 07922
USA
http://www.enslow.com

Library of Congress Cataloging-in-Publication Data

Mattern, Joanne, 1963–
    Celebrate Cinco de Mayo / Joanne Mattern.
        p. cm. — (Celebrate holidays)
    Includes bibliographical references and index.
    ISBN 0-7660-2579-9
        1. Cinco de Mayo (Mexican holiday)—Juvenile literature. 2. Mexico—
    Social life and customs—Juvenile literature. 3. Mexican Americans—
    Social life and customs—Juvenile literature. 4. Cinco de Mayo, Battle of,
    Puebla, Mexico, 1862—Juvenile literature. I. Title. II. Series.
    F1233.M435 2006
    394.262—dc22
                                                    2005028107

Printed in the United States of America

10 9 8 7 6 5 4 3 2 1

To Our Readers: We have done our best to make sure all Internet
Addresses in this book were active and appropriate when we went to press.
However, the author and the publisher have no control over and assume
no liability for the material available on those Internet sites or on other Web
sites they may link to. Any comments or suggestions can be sent by e-mail
to comments@enslow.com or to the address on the back cover.

Every effort has been made to locate all copyright holders of material used
in this book. If any errors or omissions have occurred, corrections will be
made in future editions of this book.

Illustration Credits: © 1999 Artville, LLC, p. 11; Associated Press, pp. 48,
53, 55, 56, 59, 61, 68, 71, 72, 74, 79; Associated Press, Alamogordo Daily
News, pp. 32, 64; Associated Press, Anderson Independent-Mail, p. 44;
Associated Press, The Facts, p. 46; Associated Press, Fresno Bee, p. 51;
Associated Press, The Lufkin Daily News, p. 77; Corel Corporation, p. 3;
Enslow Publishers, Inc., p. 6,   Hemera Technologies Inc., 1997–2000,
pp. 7, 13, 33, 39, 49, 57, 69; © 2006 JupiterImages, pp. 10, 12, 16, 65,
66, 83 (bottom); Library of Congress, pp. 8 (bottom), 14, 21; June Ponte-
Rogers, p. 83 (top two); Texas State Library and Archives Commission,
p. 8 (top).

Cover Illustration: Corel Corporation.

CONTENTS

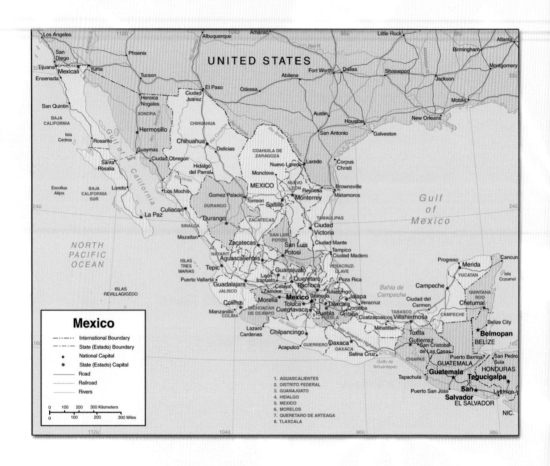

Mexico

–·–·–·–	International Boundary
–··–··–	State (Estado) Boundary
★	National Capital
●	State (Estado) Capital
———	Road
––––––	Railroad
———	Rivers

0 100 200 300 Kilometers
0 100 200 300 Miles

1. AGUASCALIENTES
2. DISTRITO FEDERAL
3. GUANAJUATO
4. HIDALGO
5. MEXICO
6. MORELOS
7. QUERETARO DE ARTEAGA
8. TLAXCALA

UNITED STATES

Los Angeles
San Diego
Tijuana
Mexicali
Yuma
Ensenada
Phoenix
Tucson
El Paso
Albuquerque
Amarillo
Little Rock
Atlanta
Birmingham
Montgomery
Jackson
Mobile
Shreveport
Dallas
Fort Worth
Abilene
Odessa
Austin
Houston
San Antonio
Galveston
New Orleans
Corpus Christi
Brownsville
Matamoros

San Quintin
BAJA CALIFORNIA
Isla Cedros
Escollos Alijos
Rosarito
Santa Rosalia
Loreto
BAJA CALIFORNIA SUR
La Paz
Gulf of California

Heroica Nogales
Ciudad Juárez
SONORA
Hermosillo
CHIHUAHUA
Chihuahua
Delicias
Guaymas
Ciudad Obregon
Los Mochis
Hidalgo del Parral
COAHUILA DE ZARAGOZA
Monclova
Nuevo Laredo
Laredo
MEXICO
NUEVO LEON
Reynosa
Monterrey
Saltillo
Gomez Palacio
Torreon
DURANGO
Durango
ZACATECAS
Culiacan
SINALOA
Mazatlan
Zacatecas
SAN LUIS POTOSI
San Luis Potosi
Ciudad Mante
TAMAULIPAS
Ciudad Victoria
Tampico
Ciudad Madero

NORTH PACIFIC OCEAN
ISLAS REVILLAGIGEDO
ISLAS TRES MARIAS
Puerto Vallarta
NAYARIT
Tepic
Aguascalientes
Guanajuato
Leon
Irapuato
JALISCO
Guadalajara
Zamora
Celaya
Queretaro
Pachuca
COLIMA
Colima
Morelia
MICHOACAN DE OCAMPO
Toluca
Mexico
Cuernavaca
Puebla
Tlaxcala
VERACRUZ-LLAVE
Poza Rica
Jalapa
Veracruz
Cordoba
Orizaba
Manzanillo
Lazaro Cardenas
Chilpancingo
GUERRERO
Acapulco
OAXACA
Oaxaca
Salina Cruz
Golfo de Tehuantepec

Gulf of Mexico
Progreso
Merida
Cancun
YUCATAN
Isla Cozumel
Campeche
QUINTANA ROO
Chetumal
CAMPECHE
Belize City
Belmopan
BELIZE
Bahia de Campeche
Ciudad del Carmen
TABASCO
Coatzacoalcos
Villahermosa
Minatitlan
Tuxtla Gutierrez
San Cristobal de las Casas
CHIAPAS
Puerto Barrios
San Pedro Sula
GUATEMALA
Guatemala
HONDURAS
Tegucigalpa
Tapachula
Puerto San Jose
San Salvador
EL SALVADOR
La Union
NIC.

Río Grande
Río Conchos
Río Verde
Río Fuerte
American Highway

Attack!

I t was May 5, 1862, and Mexico's people were under attack. The French army had invaded the country. France's leader, Napoléon III, wanted to take control of Mexico. France's large, powerful army made it seem that taking control would be very easy to do.

Early on that May morning, French general Charles Latrille Laurencez led six thousand soldiers toward the town of Puebla, just one hundred miles from Mexico City.[1] A Mexican army of about four thousand men waited to face them.

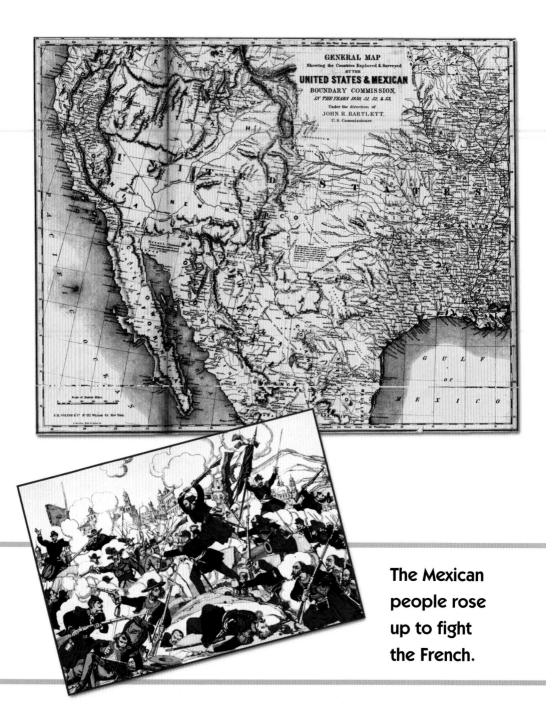

The Mexican people rose up to fight the French.

The Mexican army was led by General Ignacio Zaragoza. Zaragoza faced a seemingly impossible task. Not only was his army smaller than the French army, it was also very poorly equipped. While the French army had modern guns and cannons, the Mexicans carried long, sharp knives called machetes. The French soldiers were highly trained, while the Mexican army was made up mostly of farmers who had been called away from their fields to defend their country.[2] The two armies faced off in a field marked by uneven ground, ditches, and the remains of old adobe buildings.[3]

As the soldiers charged toward each other, thunder boomed overhead. Rain poured down, turning the battlefield into a sea of mud. The French cavalry's horses slipped and fell, unable to get their footing in the slippery mud. The rain also soaked France's supply of ammunition, making many of their guns and cannons useless.

Despite the difficulties, General Laurencez ordered his troops to charge right through the middle of Mexico's defenses. However, the uneven ground, as well as the ditches and the old building foundations made it impossible for the French to move forward. Finally, the cavalry was too exhausted to try anymore. The soldiers turned their horses around and fled.[4]

The Mexican and French armies fought hard through mud and rain.

General Zaragoza knew that his men were now in control of the battle. He ordered his troops to chase the French. The Mexican army chased them all the way to the coast. The Battle of Puebla was over. The Mexicans had won! May 5, known as Cinco de Mayo in Spanish, became one of the proudest days in Mexican history, and a holiday that has endured for more than one hundred years.

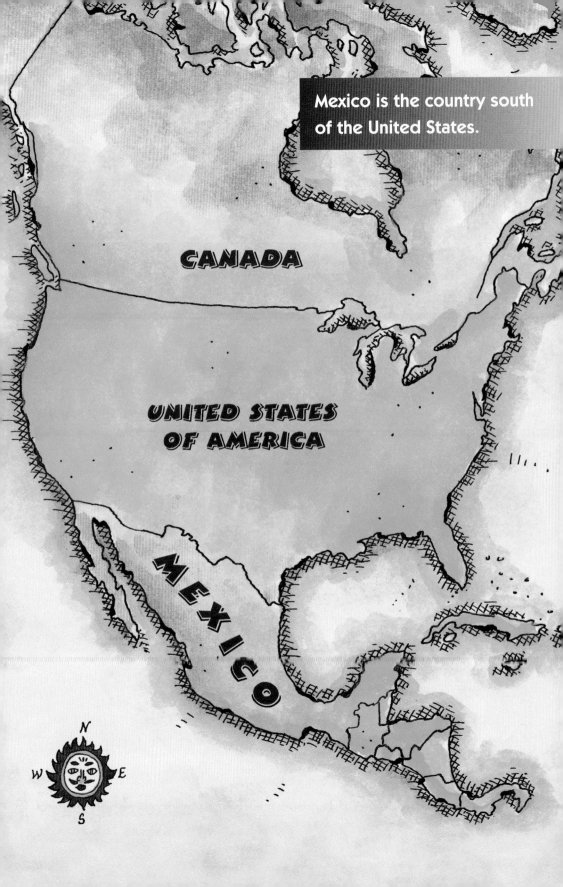

Mexico is the country south of the United States.

An ancient Mayan ruin still stands in Mexico.

The History of Cinco de Mayo

Mexico has had a long and often violent and tragic history. The country was first settled by Indian tribes some time between twelve thousand and twenty thousand years ago. Over the centuries, many different ethnic groups ruled parts of what later became Mexico. These groups included the Maya and later the Aztecs. The Aztecs were a powerful empire who ruled the country until they were defeated by a Spanish army led by Hernán Cortés in 1521. Cortés renamed the

Hernán Cortés (1485–1547)

Hernán Cortés was a Spanish explorer who is best known for conquering the Aztec empire in Mexico. He explored Santo Domingo (now the Dominican Republic) in 1504. In 1511, he helped conquer Cuba and later became mayor of the city of Santiago de Cuba. In 1518, Cortés led an expedition to Mexico.

Cortés landed on the east coast of Mexico in 1519. People in the area told him about a mighty Aztec empire. Cortés began marching inland to conquer the Aztecs. He entered their capital city, Tenochtitlán. Many of the Aztecs thought the light-skinned, bearded Spaniard was a god. The Spanish army had control of the city and took gold and other treasures. Cortés captured the Aztec leader, Montezuma, who later organized a rebellion that drove the Spanish army away. But Cortés eventually conquered the Aztecs.

Cortés built Mexico City on the ruins of Tenochtitlán. Cortés was a ruthless and cruel ruler who was much hated by the people he conquered. However, Cortés was admired in Spain and given many titles and rewards. Cortés soon returned to Spain, where he died in 1547.[1]

country New Spain, and the land was ruled by Spain for the next three hundred years. The Spanish brought their language, religion, government, and culture to Mexico.

The Spanish were often cruel rulers, and native people suffered terribly under Spanish rule. *Criollos*, or people of Spanish heritage who were born in Mexico, also resented being ruled by a foreign country, much as the American colonists resented rule by England. There were many rebellions against the Spanish government during the early 1800s. At the same time, Spain was also at war with France. This led to further instability in Mexico. Finally, an independent Mexican republic was proclaimed in 1821.[2]

Independence did not end Mexico's troubles. Mexico's land was coveted by the United States, for a variety of reasons. The United States needed space to grow crops and also had to find room for its rapidly growing population. Most of all, many United States' politicians were fervent believers in "manifest destiny," or the right to expand the country to the physical limits of the continent.[3]

During the 1820s and 1830s, many people from the United States settled in an area of Mexico known as Texas. These residents had many arguments with the Mexican government. The

This ancient Mayan ruin is a reminder of the people that lived in Mexico before the area was conquered by explorers.

arguments eventually led to war. In 1836, Texas won its independence from Mexico and began calling itself the Republic of Texas.[4]

In 1845, the Republic of Texas was annexed by the United States. However, there were disputes about exactly where the southern border of Texas was located. The United States said the border was a river called the Rio Grande, while Mexico insisted the border was the Nueces River. Finally, in April 1846, U.S. president James K. Polk sent an army to patrol the area between the two rivers. Mexico fought back, and Polk requested a declaration of war, stating that Mexico had "invaded our territory and shed American blood upon American soil."[5]

The Treaty of Guadalupe Hidalgo

On February 2, 1848, Mexican officials and a representative of President Polk signed a treaty in the city of Guadalupe, Mexico. This treaty officially ended the Mexican-American War. The Treaty of Guadalupe called for Mexico to give 55 percent of its territory to the United States. This area covered about 525,000 square miles and encompassed all or part of the present-day states of California, New Mexico, Arizona, Colorado, Nevada, Utah, and Wyoming. In exchange, Mexico received

$15 million in cash from the United States to pay for damages to Mexican property. The U.S. also agreed to assume more than $3 million in claims by U.S. citizens against the Mexican government, bringing the total payout to Mexico to just over $18 million.

The treaty also set the border between Texas and Mexico at the Rio Grande and said the United States would police its side of the border. The treaty was ratified by the U.S. Senate in March and by the Mexican government in May. American troops then left Mexico City. The war was officially over.[6,7]

A Country Divided

Mexico's troubles continued. In 1858, Mexico was caught up in a civil war, where its own people fought against each other. This civil war began as a conflict between the conservative and liberal political parties and led to the formation of two rival governments. A Zapotec Indian named Benito Juárez established his liberal government in the city of Veracruz, while conservatives ruled from Mexico City and also controlled much of the central part of the nation. Juárez's government gradually won control of the country, and Juárez became the president of the entire country in

1861.[8] Juárez's victory came at a great cost, however, as the expense of all these wars "mostly wiped out the national economy"[9] and left the country deeply in debt.

Benito Juárez

Benito Juárez was an unlikely but very well-respected and clever leader. He was born on March 21, 1806, to poor Native American farmers in the Mexican state of Oaxaca. Both of his parents died when Juárez was less than three years old, and he and his older sisters were raised by their grandparents. After they died, Juárez went to live with an uncle and took care of his flocks of sheep. His uncle took a great interest in the boy's education and sent him to school with the hope that he would become a priest.[10]

However, Juárez ran away from his uncle after one of the sheep was stolen and Juárez feared he would be blamed. He went to live in the city of Oaxaca, where he met a bookbinder named Don Antonio Salanueva. Salanueva offered to pay for Juárez's education if the boy would work for him.[11]

Juárez did study for the priesthood for a short time, but he soon discovered that his ambitions lay elsewhere. In 1829, Juárez entered a school called

The Zapotec Indians

The Zapotec Indians have lived in Mexico and other parts of Central America for more than two thousand years. Their civilization was at its height between 500 B.C. and A.D. 1500. The Zapotecs are credited with developing highly advanced forms of communication and technology. Some Zapotec myths say that these technologies came from a visitor from outer space. Drawings of this creature, called the "Astronaut," can be seen in a temple near the Sierra de Chiapas in Mexico. At its height, the Zapotec civilization flourished in Mexico's Oaxaca Valley. More than one hundred thousand people lived in the Zapotec capital city of Monte Alban and nearby areas. Today, the civilization is best known for its beautiful weavings. This ancient tradition is still practiced today.[12]

the Institute of Arts and Sciences, where he studied law and science. He went on to become a respected lawyer and politician in Oaxaca. His clients were some of the region's poorest residents, and Juárez soon came to believe that the powers of the upper classes needed to be cut back in order for the underprivileged to have a better life. In 1841, Juárez became a judge. Later, he served as a state legislator and a congressman. In 1847, he became

Benito Juárez became a great Mexican leader.
He was elected president of Mexico in 1858.

the governor of Oaxaca. Juárez soon gained national attention for his policies, which featured "public spirit, fairness, honesty, and thrift."[13]

When Juárez's term as governor ended in 1852, he returned to the Institute of Arts and Sciences as the school's director. Trouble lay ahead, however. While he was governor, he had refused a request for asylum by former president Antonio Lopez de Santa Anna, who was fleeing after a defeat by U.S. troops during the Mexican-American War. After Santa Anna returned to the presidency in 1853, he had Juárez arrested and exiled to Havana, Cuba. Juárez soon made his way to the United States and lived in New Orleans, where many other Mexican exiles had settled. The exiles eventually overthrew Santa Anna in 1854, and Juárez returned to power. Juárez held many important posts in the new government. Finally, in 1858, Juárez was elected president.[14]

Juárez "inherited a bankrupt and divided nation."[15] He realized that Mexico was so poor, it could not repay the vast amounts of money it had borrowed from European countries. On July 17, 1861, Juárez announced that it would not repay any foreign loans for the next two years.[16]

Santa Anna

Antonio Lopez de Santa Anna was the most important figure in Mexican politics for most of the nineteenth century. He was born in Veracruz, Mexico, in 1794 and entered the army at age sixteen. In 1821, he and other army officers helped install Augustin de Iturbe as Mexico's president. In 1833, after years of political influence, Santa Anna was elected president of Mexico by a huge margin. However, the next twenty-two years were chaotic. During this time, Mexico had thirty-six different changes in leadership, and Santa Anna was president eleven times. Things were so confusing that, in 1835, Santa Anna led a military uprising against his own government.

In 1835, Santa Anna led the Mexican army against the Texans and became notorious for wiping out all the U.S. defenders of the fort called the Alamo. Later, in 1838, Santa Anna defeated a French force trying to invade Veracruz. Santa Anna lost part of his left leg during this battle, which further increased his status as a war hero. Santa Anna remained a powerful figure in Mexico until 1853, when he was chased out of office for the final time. He died in 1876.[17]

War With France

Great Britain, Spain, and France's governments were furious when they heard about Juárez's decision. To get their money, these countries decided to invade Mexico. Armies from England, France, and Spain landed in Veracruz, a city on the eastern shore of Mexico, in December 1861. Once again, Mexico was in terrible danger.

The European armies planned to seize the customs house in Veracruz and take Mexico's customs payments as payment for the country's debt. At the same time, diplomats for Spain and Great Britain negotiated with Juárez to settle the financial dispute. An agreement was reached in April 1862, and Spain and Great Britain's armies headed home.[18]

France, however, had a different plan. At that time, France was ruled by a man named Napoléon III. Napoléon III was nervous about how big and powerful the United States had become. He thought that a strong French presence in North America would keep the United States from becoming even more powerful. Napoléon decided that making Mexico part of the French empire was the answer to his problems. Mexico's refusal to repay French loans gave him the perfect excuse to conquer the country.

Napoléon III (1808–1873)

Charles Louis Napoléon Bonaparte was born in Paris in 1808. He was the third son of King Louis and Queen Hortense of Holland. The famous Napoléon Bonaparte was his uncle. Charles' family wanted him to restore the honor and glory of the Bonaparte family, which had lost power. Charles led several armed attempts to overthrow King Louis Philippe of France. The attempts were unsuccessful, and Charles was imprisoned for a time. Finally, King Louis Philippe lost the throne in 1848, and Napoléon III was elected president of the new French government. Although he was elected to just a four-year term, Napoléon declared himself a dictator in 1851. Since Napoléon I's son had been known as Napoléon II, Charles took on the title Napoléon III to continue the most famous name of the Bonaparte family.

Napoléon III wanted France to be an important world power, and he led the country into several wars to achieve this goal. Between 1854 and 1856, France fought alongside Great Britain in the Crimean War to stop Russian advancement. In 1859, France fought against Sardinia to keep Austria out of Italy. Napoléon III was defeated and surrendered to the Germans during the Franco-Prussian War in 1870. He died in exile in England in 1873.[19]

As the French army marched from Veracruz toward the capital, Mexico City, President Juárez asked the United States for help. Relations had improved between the two nations since the end of the Mexican-American War, and America's president, Abraham Lincoln, was sympathetic to the Mexican cause. However, the United States was in the middle of its own Civil War and could not send any aid.[20] Mexico was on its own. President Juárez remained defiant and determined to protect his country. He stated, "The Imperial Government [France] will not succeed in subduing the Mexicans, and its armies will not have a single day of peace . . . we must stop them, not only for our country but for the respect of the sovereignty of the nations."[21]

The Battle of Puebla

On May 5, 1862, six thousand French soldiers moved in to capture the forts of Loreto and Guadalupe in the town of Puebla de Los Angeles.[22] They were met by a Mexican army led by General Ignacio Zaragoza. Zaragoza's army had about four thousand men. His soldiers were not only outnumbered, they were poorly trained and did not have very good equipment. Instead of guns and cannons like the French soldiers, the Mexicans

Ignacio Zaragoza

Ignacio Zaragoza was born in 1829. He joined the army at a young age and eventually became a general. Zaragoza always fought to preserve Mexico's efforts to create a democratic government.

In April 1861, President Benito Juárez appointed Zaragoza minister of war and minister of the navy. When the French invaded Mexico in 1862, Zaragoza led a determined band of farmers-turned-soldiers against the larger French army at the Battle of Puebla. Using cleverness and skill, Zaragoza's smaller army defeated the French and won the battle. Zaragoza became a national hero. However, he became ill with typhoid fever and died in Puebla on September 8, 1862. Juárez renamed the city after him. Later, a statue was erected in his honor, and many streets, schools, and plazas have been named after Zaragoza.[23]

had knives, swords, spears, and farm tools. Some soldiers only carried sticks and rocks.

General Zaragoza knew that he had several advantages over the French army. He and his men knew the land better than the French did. Zaragoza also had some tricks up his sleeve. He told the French general he would surrender, then sent a troop of soldiers on a surprise attack against the French. Zaragoza also had his soldiers create a stampede of cattle toward the French troops. This split the French forces in half and made it harder for the French to fight.

Bad weather also helped the Mexican army. Heavy rain made the battlefield muddy and soggy. French cannons and supply carts sank in the mud. Soldiers and horses could not move through the wet ground. Gunpowder for French guns and cannons got so wet, it would not work.

After four hours of fierce fighting, the Mexican army defeated the French, even though the French army was much larger, well armed, and made up of professionally trained soldiers.[24] More than a thousand French soldiers were dead.[25] The French had to retreat.

France's Defeat

Word of Mexico's triumph spread across the country. The Mexican people were filled with pride. The battle became "a striking example of determination, courage, and ingenuity against overwhelming odds."[26] Zaragoza became such a hero that the town of Puebla de Los Angeles was renamed Puebla de Zaragoza in his honor.[27]

France may have lost the Battle of Puebla, but they would go on to win the war. Napoléon III sent thirty thousand more soldiers to Mexico. The French army soon took control of Mexico City. President Juárez fled to northern Mexico, leaving the country in the hands of the French. Napoléon III appointed an Austrian named Maximilian to be the new emperor of Mexico. Maximilian was an archduke in Austria and an admiral in the Austrian navy.[28] He was distantly related to Napoléon III and very good friends with the French ruler, who decided he would be a good choice to rule this outpost of the French empire.[29]

French control of Mexico did not last very long. Although the United States was unable to help Mexico during the U.S. Civil War (1861–1865), President Lincoln was very concerned about what was going on there. After the Civil War ended, the American government was able to assist Mexico. It sent money and aid to President Juárez, who had remained in northern Mexico to rebuild his army. Several thousand soldiers also traveled from the United States to Mexico to help defend the nation.

Mexico's refusal to give up, combined with the soldiers and aid from the United States, were too much for France. On January 15, 1866, Napoléon III announced the end of the French occupation of Mexico and began withdrawing French troops.[31] Maximilian remained in Mexico until he finally

The United States Civil War

Between 1861 and 1865, the United States was torn apart in a conflict known as the Civil War. The war started as a dispute between the northern and southern states about economics, party politics, state power versus federal authority, and slavery. When Abraham Lincoln was elected president of the United States in 1860, Southern states decided to leave, or secede, from the nation. The first state to do so was South Carolina. By February 7, 1861, seven states had seceded and adopted a new constitution. They called themselves the Confederate States of America.

On April 12, 1861, the civil war officially began when federal troops (known as the Union) were fired upon at Fort Sumter in Charleston, South Carolina. The conflict escalated and led to major battles, fought mostly in the Southern states. During the war, Lincoln issued his famous Emancipation Proclamation, which freed the slaves. Although the Confederacy won many of the early battles, the Union eventually defeated the Southern states. In April 1865, Confederate general Robert E. Lee surrendered at Appomattox Court House in Virginia. Although a few battles were fought after that date, Lee's surrender is considered to be the end of the war.[30]

surrendered to Benito Juárez in 1867. Juárez had Maximilian executed on June 19, 1867.[32] Once again, Juárez was the president of Mexico, and the Mexican people were free.

Despite the fact that the Battle of Puebla did not end the war against France, the Mexican people never forgot the importance of May 5, 1862. They remembered and celebrated how an outnumbered and poorly trained army made up of native Mexicans could defeat one of the most powerful countries in the world. Even while Maximilian was their emperor and the French continued to rule the nation, Mexicans celebrated Cinco de Mayo. The victory they achieved that day gave the Mexican people confidence to overthrow the French and finally take control of their destiny.

Cultural Significance of Cinco de Mayo

Cinco de Mayo has become an important cultural event for Mexicans. This is true both of Mexicans in Mexico as well as those living in the United States. The holiday celebrates more than just a victory in battle. It also gives Mexicans a chance to celebrate national pride. Also, even though the battle on May 5, 1862, did not end the French occupation, it showed Mexicans that they had a chance to be independent and free. The battle showed the world that Mexico was willing to defend itself against any foreign power. "The victory demonstrated to ordinary Mexican citizens that they could repel superior fighting power. It instilled national pride, improved the international stature of President Juárez, and discouraged further . . . invasion of Mexico and Latin America."[1] Cinco de Mayo is also significant to all North Americans because it was the last time any foreign nation's army set foot in a North American country.

Mexico and the United States

Cinco de Mayo also became a day for Mexico and the United States to celebrate their friendship. The large Mexican population in the United States has led to close ties between the two nations. The United States and Mexico have also helped each other financially and militarily over the years.

Although Cinco de Mayo was an important day for Mexico and her people, it did not become a major holiday right away. The holiday's status as a major fiesta, or party, did not happen in Mexico either. Instead, Cinco de Mayo became a large commercial event in the United States.

At first, Cinco de Mayo was a cultural celebration that provided a way for Mexicans living in California to show their love and unity with their homeland. A year after the Battle of Puebla, while Mexico was still fighting against the French occupation, a Mexican businessman in San Francisco sponsored a Cinco de Mayo dance.[2] For the next ninety years, Cinco de Mayo was celebrated on a fairly small scale in the United States. Mexican cultural groups held private dances. Mexican-American community leaders made speeches about the battle and its importance, and Mexican communities held parades. Dancers performed special Mexican *folklorico* dances. Throughout the 1950s, Cinco de Mayo was a local celebration, and usually only residents of a city's Mexican-American community were interested enough to take part.[3]

The Move for Civil Rights

Things began to change during the 1960s. During this decade, many ethnic groups demanded more civil rights. "Like the African American community, the Latino community in the United States began to demand equality and to fight against all forms of discrimination. . . . From this growing self-awareness grew the Chicano movement, an effort by Mexican Americans to re-embrace their indigenous roots and recognize the struggle of native people in Mexico against the Spanish conquistadors and other European invaders."[4]

The Civil Rights Movement

The 1950s and 1960s saw the rise of the American civil rights movement. The goal of this movement was to achieve equality for all Americans. Until the 1950s, most states, particularly in the South, had laws that made sure African Americans were treated as second-class citizens. African Americans could not stay in white hotels or eat in white restaurants. They could not swim in public pools used by white people and had to sit in certain seats or cars on public buses and trains. Children had to attend separate schools. The laws even made it difficult for African Americans to vote. This process of legal separation was called segregation.

In 1954, the Supreme Court declared school segregation to be illegal. Then, in 1955, Rosa Parks refused to give up her seat to a white man on a public bus in Montgomery, Alabama. Her act of defiance led to a citywide bus boycott that lasted more than a year. The Supreme Court eventually declared that segregated buses were illegal. The Montgomery bus boycott also brought national attention to one of its leaders, the Reverend Martin Luther King, Jr. King preached a method of nonviolence and patience to win civil rights for all.

> Through the 1950s and 1960s, civil actions and public outcry slowly changed laws. Public places and schools were integrated. The Voting Rights Act was passed to remove barriers to voting.
>
> During the late 1960s, the civil rights movement began to be more violent. King's idea of nonviolent protest was viewed by some as too gentle and ineffective. After King was assassinated in 1968, riots broke out in many major cities. In time, legal civil rights became a reality for all Americans.[5]

Cinco de Mayo celebrations were an excellent way for Mexican-Americans to celebrate their heritage and recall the glory of the Battle of Puebla, when they had defeated a much more powerful army.

During the 1960s, Mexican Americans began looking for a celebration that would reflect their history and cultural heritage.[6] Cinco de Mayo seemed like a good choice.

Mexican Independence Day

Just as July 4 is celebrated as the United States' Independence Day, September 16 is Mexico's

Independence Day. Just as the United States declared their independence several years before the nation actually won its freedom, Mexico also faced many years of struggle before their independence was a reality.

In 1810, many Mexicans wanted to start a revolution to break free of their ruler, Spain. One of the revolutionary leaders was a priest named Father Miguel Hidalgo, from the town of Delores. The Spanish government found out that Hidalgo was making weapons and training the people of his church how to fight. Spanish officials ordered Hidalgo's arrest, but the priest found out what was happening before the soldiers arrived. Late on the night of September 15, 1810, he rang a bell to call his congregation together. When everyone arrived, Father Hidalgo gave a speech that became known as the Grito de Delores (Tears of Sorrow). He encouraged the people to fight, shouting, "*Viva Mexico!*" ("Long live Mexico!") and "*Viva la independencia!*" ("Long live independence!"). Hidalgo's people responded and fought many battles against the Spanish soldiers. The revolutionary army traveled all the way to Mexico City before they were finally defeated by the Spaniards. Father Hidalgo was captured and killed, but his Grito de Delores lived on as a battle cry for Mexican independence.

Finally, eleven years later, in 1821, the country won its freedom.

Today, September 16 is celebrated as Independence Day throughout Mexico. Most towns hold large parties, or fiestas. These fiestas can include parades, music, dancing, special foods, bullfights, rodeos, and fireworks. Town squares are decorated in Mexico's national colors of red, white, and green, and the Mexican flag is everywhere. The festivities actually start on September 15, in Mexico City, the capital of Mexico. Here the Mexican president appears in public at eleven o'clock at night to ring the same bell that Father Hidalgo rang to call his people together. Then the president reads the Grito de Delores, and the people shout back, "*Viva Mexico! Viva la independencia!*"[7]

Although September 16 was the actual anniversary of the date Mexico achieved independence, May 5 remained a vital and cherished day in Mexican history. It was a day of pride in the nation's accomplishments, and many people

The Mexican flag is a symbol of pride for many people.

found it to be a more significant cause for celebration than the actual independence day. Since Mexicans were a minority group in the United States, they sensed a connection to the out-numbered Mexican army defeating a more powerful nation at the Battle of Puebla.

Much of the great social change that occurred during the 1960s came about because of student activists and public protests against the unfair treatment of African Americans, Chicanos (Hispanics), women, and other marginalized groups. An important factor in Cinco de Mayo's popularity in the United States was the Chicano student movement of the late 1960s.[8] These students took their cues from other student-led protests and looked for a day they could celebrate their own ancestry. Although Mexican Independence Day, which is celebrated on September 16, seemed the most logical choice, it was too early in the school year for students to organize celebrations. Instead, Cinco de Mayo was chosen as a day of national pride.[9] Over the years, the holiday spread from universities with a large Mexican population to mainstream communities throughout the south-western part of the United States.[10] For Hispanics struggling to fight segregation, illegal deportations, and numerous human rights violations, "the memory of Puebla continued to inspire strength and the determination to control our destiny with dignity."[11]

The Government Steps In

The 1960s was a time of greater public awareness toward the needs of ethnic groups in the United States. There was a great deal of government effort to reach out to ethnic groups, especially those who were members of poor or disadvantaged communities. In 1964, the U.S. Congress passed the Civil Rights Act, and in 1965, the Elementary and Secondary Schools Education Act.[12] Both of these acts mandated the desegregation of public schools and increased public funding for marginalized ethnic communities.

In 1968, the U.S. government took another step toward recognizing the needs of ethnic groups when it passed the Bilingual Education Act.[13] This act mandated schools to provide bilingual education programs. "It authorized resources to support educational programs, to train teachers and aides, to develop and disseminate instructional materials, and to encourage parental involvement."[14] The most lasting effect of the new law was to give equal education to students who

In the United States, many students learn about the significance of Cinco de Mayo in school. This girl is getting help from her teacher with a project.

that occurred on May 5. Many Mexicans feel that American celebrations do not put enough focus on the seriousness of the battle the holiday commemorates. Some even believe that the day should only be a Mexican holiday.[20] However, this view ignores the significance the Mexican victory at the Battle of Puebla has for the United States. Mexico's determination to escape from French rule had important consequences in U.S. history as well. At the time of the Battle of Puebla, the United States was in the middle of the Civil War. If the French had stayed in power in Mexico, they would have spread north and eventually made a challenge to the United States. "If Puebla had not delayed the advance of the French, Lincoln would have found a French army at the border of a divided United States. A force ready to finance and arm the Confederacy. Instead, the United States would reunite and become the most powerful army in the world."[21]

Cinco de Mayo is also important in the United States because of the large number of Mexican-Americans in the population. In 2003, there were about 25.3 million people living in the United States who were of Mexican origin, making up 9 percent of the U.S. total population. About 16.6 million Mexican Americans live in California

These Texan students wave Mexican flags after performing their version of a battle re-enactment for Mexican independence. They learn about Mexican Independence Day and Cinco de Mayo in their schools.

or Texas, making up one third of the residents of these two states.[22] Clearly, Mexican-Americans are an important part of U.S. culture, especially in the Southwest.

Another common misconception is that Cinco de Mayo celebrates Mexico's independence from Spain, just as July 4 celebrates the United States' independence from Great Britain. This confusion and lack of information is very annoying to Mexicans and other people who want the true meaning of the day to be remembered. However, a more positive view is that Cinco de Mayo has become a day to celebrate pride, independence, and freedom.

Mexicans take part in the re-enactment of the famous Cinco de Mayo battle in Mexico.

4

Who Celebrates Cinco de Mayo?

It is ironic that Cinco de Mayo has become a bigger holiday in the United States than it is in Mexico. Although it is a national holiday in Mexico, Cinco de Mayo is not celebrated on a large scale throughout the country. The largest celebrations take place in the state of Puebla, where the important battle occurred, but celebrations are not as widespread in other parts of the country. The holiday is noted throughout the country, but there are different levels of enthusiasm and celebration.[1]

Celebrations in Mexico

In Puebla, Mexico, however, celebrations are much more widespread. These celebrations include military parades that honor soldiers and civilians who gave their lives in defense of their country. Schools take part in these parades as well, sending marching bands to the festivities. These parades are so popular that people get up very early so they can find a good spot on the street to watch the parade pass by.[2]

Mexico City also has a Cinco de Mayo celebration. In a neighborhood called Peñon de los Baños, residents organize a play re-enacting the Battle of Puebla. Some residents play the French invaders, while others portray the Mexican army.[3] The Mexican president gives a speech in Mexico City that is broadcast to the nation on television.[4]

Other cities hold celebrations in the *zócalo*, or central plaza. These celebrations can include music, dancing, street fairs, carnivals, and lots of Mexican food.[5] Often a piñata is set up for the children to play with. Children are blindfolded and try to hit the piñata with a stick to break it. Once the piñata is broken, the children rush forward to claim the candy inside. At the end of the day, fireworks light up the sky in a colorful and noisy

This couple performs a traditional Mexican dance during a celebration in California.

end to the festivities as everyone yells, "Viva Mexico! Long live Mexico!"[6]

Cinco de Mayo in the United States

Although Cinco de Mayo is certainly celebrated in Mexico, it is a much bigger holiday in the United States. This is especially true in the western and southwestern part of the country. States such as Texas, Arizona, New Mexico, and California have large Mexican populations, so they were the first areas to celebrate Cinco de Mayo on a large scale, and are still places where Cinco de Mayo is most popular.

The Mexican population in the United States is not the only reason that Cinco de Mayo has become popular there. Clever marketing by several different industries also encouraged people throughout the nation to celebrate this holiday.[7] Food and beverage companies market Mexican products such as tortillas and Mexican beer to be used for Cinco de Mayo celebrations, and super-markets feature these products to increase sales. Party-supply stores also feature holiday-themed banners, tableware, and other products in Mexico's national colors of red, white, and green to increase their sales.[8]

This boy takes a swing at a piñata his class made in school in Missouri.

In 2005, a South Florida newspaper called the *Sun-Sentinel* said Cinco de Mayo, as celebrated in the United States today, bore little resemblance to the battle or even the cultural heritage the day was meant to commemorate. Author Sandra Hernandez said, "Almost 150 years later, the memory of the courageous battle had faded, replaced with slick marketing campaigns and novel alcohol-related items ranging from coasters to the ever-popular inflatable beer can."[9]

Amon Hoang-Rappaport, a spokesman for the Marin Institute, a watchdog for the alcohol industry, agrees with Hernandez. "What was once a source of cultural pride has been reduced to a binge drinking holiday, thanks to the alcohol industry," Hoang-Rappaport says.[10]

It is not hard to figure out why the advertising industry wants to reach out to Hispanics. This group is the fastest growing demographic group in the United States and was spent an estimated $700 billion in 2005.[11] Cinco de Mayo creates "a commercial entry point for people who want to penetrate the Latino market," according to Felix Gutierrez, a journalism professor at the University of Southern California's Annenberg School for Communication. "They want to get money out of these communities."[12]

A man sells Mexican flags on a street in Denver, Colorado, before Cinco de Mayo celebrations.

It is interesting to note that Cinco de Mayo is not a federal holiday in the United States, in the sense that Memorial Day, the Fourth of July, Labor Day, or Presidents' Day are. However, it is the biggest Mexican celebration in the United States and, despite the commercialization, still a source of enjoyment and pride. Along with celebrating Mexico's culture and history and promoting national and ethnic pride, Cinco de Mayo allows America's many different ethnic groups to learn about, share, and enjoy Mexico's culture.

Cinco de Mayo is a time for celebration and dancing. This man performs in Los Angeles, California, at a Cinco de Mayo fiesta.

Symbols of Cinco de Mayo

Cinco de Mayo celebrations feature several important aspects of Mexico's culture. Traditional music, dancing, costumes, and food are all vital parts of any Cinco de Mayo celebration.

Music

Music has been an important feature of Mexican life and culture since ancient times. So it is no surprise that music is also one of the most important features of a Cinco de Mayo fiesta. A style of music known as *mariachi* is played at these celebrations. Mariachi had its beginnings during the days when Spain ruled Mexico, and the music is a combination of Mexican folk music set to the beat of African rhythms.[1] When Mexico was under Spain's control, orchestras provided music for theatrical presentations. "The typical Spanish theatrical orchestra of the sixteenth, seventeenth, and eighteenth centuries was comprised of violins [usually two], harp, and guitars [or guitar variants]."[2] During the nineteenth century, Mexicans came up with their own version of the Spanish orchestra. The Mexican orchestra became known as "mariachi." Music historians believe that the mariachi we know today first developed in the town of Cocula, in the Mexican state of Jalisco.[3] These orchestras included violins, harp, and guitars. They played a type of music called *son* which featured a mixture of folk traditions from Spain, Mexico, and Africa.[4] The music featured contrasting sounds from the different instruments, creating unusual and lively rhythms and melodies.

Today's mariachi bands consist of "five to 14 or more musicians who rely on five instruments: a guitar, violin, trumpet, *guitarron* [a large bass guitar], and *vihuela* [a small guitar with a curved back]."[5]

These boys tune their instruments before playing. The big instrument is a guitarron. The smaller one is a vihuela.

Dance

From the beginning, mariachi music was meant to be danced to. Mexican dance music is known as folklorico. These dances are graceful, lively, and full of expression. Although folklorico is the national dance of Mexico, different styles of dance are popular in different parts of the country. Dances from each Mexican state have their own style of movement, costumes, and music.[6] No matter where the dance originates, each is highly symbolic and tells a story. For example, "La Bamba" from Veracruz is a popular wedding song, while "Los Machates" from the state of Jalisco allows men to show off their swordsmanship.[7] Dancers often incorporate objects into their dances, such as ribbons or fans.[8]

The traditional dance connected with mariachi is called *zapateado*. Zapateado is the rhythmic stamping and tapping of the heels featured in Spanish dancing. "When dancing the zapateado, the performers skillfully drive the heels of their boots or shoes into the dance floor, pounding out swift, often syncopated rhythms which complement the different rhythm of the musical instruments."[9] Sometimes, the dancers pound their feet so hard that they actually cause the floor

These folkloric dancers perform a traditional Mexican dance in downtown Los Angeles, California.

to splinter! Today, the zapateado is an important part of Cinco de Mayo celebrations.

Another popular dance that is often seen at Cinco de Mayo fiestas is the Mexican hat dance, or the *jarabe tapatio.* This dance has been called "the national folk dance of Mexico."[10] The dance features a man and a woman and is an expression

The Mexican Revolution

Jarabe tapatio had its origins as an expression of national unity during the Mexican Revolution that tore the country apart between 1910 and 1920. The conflict began after a rebel group led by Francisco Ignacio Madero opposed the leadership of President Porfirio Diaz, who many considered to be a dictator. In 1911, Diaz resigned and Madero became president. However, he wanted to change the country through political reform, not revolution, which disappointed some of his more radical followers. These radicals united behind two leaders, Emiliano Zapata and Francisco "Pancho" Villa.[13]

Violence escalated, and Madero was replaced by Victoriano Huerta in 1913. Four days after he took office, Huerta had Madero murdered.[14] Huerta called out the Mexican army to fight the rebels, but he was forced to resign in 1914 after U.S. president Woodrow Wilson sent the navy into Veracruz to prevent the delivery of weapons to Huerta's army.[15]

The rebels also faced fighting within their ranks. Venustiano Carranza, the governor of the state of Coahuila, had differences with Zapata and Villa and fought against them. Eventually, Villa and Zapata were forced out of Mexico City, and Carranza took control. Carranza insisted that the United States recognize his authority. In August 1915, a commission of eight Latin American countries and the United States recognized Carranza as the lawful leader of Mexico.[16] Although he drafted a new constitution, Carranza could not keep control of the country. In 1920, three generals revolted against Carranza and killed him. One of the generals, Alvaro Obregón, was elected president in 1920. The United States supported Obregón, and the civil war finally came to an end.[17]

of love between them. It is known as the Mexican hat dance because male dancers throw their hats into the middle of a circle and dance around them with quick, lively steps.[11]

The dance known as jarabe tapatio was very popular during and after the Mexican Revolution. Around 1930, the jarabe tapatio became internationally known when the great Russian ballerina Anna Pavlova included the dance in her permanent repertoire of performances.[12]

Costumes

Costumes are another important part of Cinco de Mayo celebrations. Members of mariachi bands

Jarabe tapatio was a popular dance during the Mexican Revolution. These dancers perform it during a New Mexico Cinco de Mayo celebration.

wear special outfits: "a waist-length jacket and tightly fitted wool pants which open slightly at the ankle to fit over a short riding boot. Both pants and jacket are often ornamented with embroidery, intricately cut leather designs, or silver buttons in a variety of shapes."[18]

Folklorico dancers also wear elaborate costumes. These costumes are symbols of Mexican culture.[19] Women wear long skirts with colorful silk and ribbons and sparkling sequins sewn on. Often, these skirts are covered with so many sequins that it is impossible to see the fabric underneath. The colorful skirts are paired with white, loose-fitting, peasant-style blouses. This outfit comes from the clothes worn by peasant women

A sombrero

during the early to mid-1800s.[20] These clothes were also worn by women called *soldaderos*, who followed the army to cook and clean for them at the Battle of Puebla and other battles in the war against France.[21] Men also wear traditional costumes consisting of ruffled shirts, black jackets, and large hats called sombreros.

There are many types of Mexican foods. Tacos are a popular dish.

Food

Food is another important part of Cinco de Mayo celebrations. People enjoy traditional Mexican foods, including tortillas, chalupas, and tamales. Tortillas are thin, flat disks made from corn or wheat flour and baked on a hot surface. They can be filled with many different foods, including meats and vegetables. A chalupa is a boat-shaped, fried tortilla filled with meat and garnished with sauce, cheese, lettuce, and onions. A tamale is a very popular Mexican dish. It is made of chopped meat, crushed peppers, and spices wrapped in corn husks. The husks are then spread with a special corn dough called masa and steamed. On Cinco de Mayo, these foods are enjoyed at public fiestas and also shared by families and friends at home or in restaurants.

In a Battle of Puebla re-enactment, the "French" troops advance on Mexican territory. The event takes place in Mexico every year.

Cinco de Mayo Today

Cinco de Mayo is an important holiday in both Mexico and the United States, but it is celebrated very differently in the two countries. In Mexico, Cinco de Mayo is a national holiday. Celebrations are organized by the government and focus more on the events of the Battle of Puebla. In the United States, celebrations are organized by community organizations and focus more on celebrating Mexican pride through a festive party.

The Holiday in Mexico

The most elaborate Cinco de Mayo celebrations in Mexico take place in the state of Puebla. The day's events usually start with a parade that steps off about eleven o'clock in the morning. The marchers include several marching bands, as well as people dressed up as Mexican and French soldiers and generals. These "soldiers" carry old-fashioned weapons, such as machetes and old gunpowder rifles.[1] Women also march in the parade to represent the women who traveled with the army to care for the soldiers. Men and women often wear old-fashioned clothes as part of the celebration too. Men wear an outfit called a *charro*. A charro includes a short jacket called a *bolero*, a white shirt, black pants with big silver or gold buttons down the legs, and boots with spurs.[2] Some men dress up like Benito Juárez in a black suit with a cape and a tall black hat.[3] Women wear an outfit called *China Poblana*. This costume includes a long, red and green skirt decorated with sequins and beads, a short-sleeved white blouse, and a silk shawl.[4]

By the time the parade reaches the city square, it is afternoon. There the Battle of Puebla takes place again. The soldiers re-enact the battle, complete with cannons, smoke, and lots of

Actors dressed as Zapotec Indians defend a fort
during a re-enactment of the Battle of Puebla.

Even today, in the town of Puebla, Mexico, people dress up and re-enact the Battle of Puebla.

shouting. At nightfall, men representing the Mexican and French generals meet for a sword battle. Of course, the Mexican general always wins! Cinco de Mayo events in Puebla also include speeches by government officials and ceremonies to honor those who fought and died in the Battle of Puebla.

The Mexican celebration of Cinco de Mayo is a time for fun too! There is a public festival, or fiesta, for everyone to enjoy. The fiesta includes many different events. Some of these events are mariachi music, dancing, games, and bullfights. Piñatas stuffed with candy are hung for children to smash open. Traditional foods, such as tamales, tortillas, and *mole poblano* (a thick spicy sauce made from more than forty ingredients and spread on top of turkey or chicken and red rice)[5] are cooked and eaten outdoors, and the town is decorated with Mexican flags and banners showing Mexico's national colors: green, white, and red. When darkness falls, the fiesta ends with a display of fireworks.[6]

The Holiday in the United States

In the United States, Cinco de Mayo celebrations take a slightly different course. The historical significance of the day—the victory at the Battle of Puebla—is not usually remembered. Instead, the day is a celebration of Mexican pride.

Los Angeles, California

One very popular Cinco de Mayo celebration in the United States is the L.A. Fiesta Broadway, which is held in Los Angeles, California. This city has the

The L.A. Fiesta Broadway attracts many visitors. There is music, food, and many other things to see and do.

largest Latino population in the United States.[7] The fiesta was established in 1989. This daylong event attracts up to five hundred thousand participants and covers thirty-six square blocks in the downtown part of the city. L.A. Fiesta Broadway features concerts by Latino bands, a sports center, a health expo, and a children's art workshop. The fiesta also features food vendors who raise money for nonprofit groups such as school and community organizations, and an art and essay contest for area students. Participants wear traditional Mexican clothing. A stage is set up on the steps of City Hall and decorated with a picture of General Zaragoza. The mayor makes a speech in Spanish, and important Mexican officials are guests of honor.[8] The day is billed as an event "dedicated to the working Latino family that looks forward to commemorating their heritage and traditions in a cultural, artistic, and safe environment on the famous downtown Los Angeles Broadway corridor."[9]

It is important to note that even though L.A. Fiesta Broadway is a cultural event, it was started for commercial reasons. In the late 1980s, the Spanish-language television network Univision was looking for a way to reach Los Angeles' large Latino population. The network already sponsored a similar cultural event, the Calle Ocho festival in Miami, which was geared to that city's large Cuban population. The network approached Los Angeles mayor Tom Bradley and asked the city to cosponsor the event with them. Since then, L.A. Fiesta Broadway has found local sponsors to cover its $1 million budget. In the words of former Univision executive and event planner Larry Gonzalez, the fiesta bills itself as "an event that recognized the rich contributions that the Mexican American culture has made to the city and that also brought together the broader community. . . . the most efficient and nonthreatening way to break down barriers is through music, food, and culture."[10]

San Marcos, Texas

San Marcos, Texas, also has a large and well-organized community celebration of Cinco de Mayo. This city's event is called Viva! Cinco de Mayo and is held in the city's historical district. It features a parade, musical performances by many mariachi bands and folklorico dancers, and two beauty pageants that award scholarships toward the winners' college educations.[11] San Marcos is not the only city in Texas that celebrates Cinco de Mayo. Austin and San Antonio both celebrate the holiday with festivals and parades.

Many states hold Cinco de Mayo celebrations.
This woman makes fajitas in a park in Texas.

Denver, Colorado

The Cinco de Mayo celebration in Denver, Colorado, has been called the largest Cinco de Mayo festival in the United States. More than five hundred thousand people attend the event, which is held at the city's Civic Center Park. The festival started as a street fair in the mid-1980s and grew into a two-day festival dedicated to celebrating Mexican culture.[12] The festival includes a parade, music, dancing, a carnival, demonstrations of Mexican and Native American arts and crafts, traditional food, and cultural exhibits.[13]

Around the United States

Other communities also celebrate Cinco de Mayo. San Antonio and Houston, Texas, and Chicago, Illinois all hold large public festivals. San Diego, which is near the Mexican border, holds an annual Fiesta Cinco de Mayo in its historic Old Town district. This event attracts more than one hundred thousand visitors each year and features three days of music, dancing, and entertainment, as well as cultural and historic exhibits, re-enactments of the Battle of Puebla, and many different kinds of authentic Mexican food.[14]

Large Cinco de Mayo celebrations are not as common in northern cities, and most began more

A dancer performs a Latin dance during a Cinco de Mayo program at an Oklahoma City, Oklahoma, school.

recently than celebrations in the Southwest. New York City, for example, did not have an official Cinco de Mayo celebration until 2002. That year, the Committee for National Mexican Holidays and Casa Puebla organized a celebration at Flushing Park in Queens, one of New York City's five boroughs. The celebration featured popular Mexican entertainers and was hailed as a great way to showcase Mexican culture to the city. The event was a big success and has been held every year since.[15]

The Significance of Cinco de Mayo

Community groups in other cities and towns sponsor fiestas where people can gather to enjoy traditional Mexican foods, music, and dancing. Throughout the United States, families and friends also gather for private celebrations in homes and restaurants.

Cinco de Mayo has taken an interesting twist in the United States. What started as a day to commemorate a stunning and inspiring victory in battle has become a cultural event that celebrates Mexico's beautiful traditions and creates ethnic pride. Event planner Larry Gonzalez notes that "Cinco de Mayo celebrations are very much a product of the Chicano movement and were popularized by Latinos in California. But it has also reached areas like New York and Miami, where it has become as mainstream as St. Patrick's Day. It is important that these communities also understand the significance of Cinco de Mayo and what the battle represented."[16]

No matter how it is celebrated, Cinco de Mayo remains a day of pride for Mexicans, and a day to celebrate and honor bravery and determination against overwhelming odds. As Cinco de Mayo becomes more popular throughout the United States, this fiesta provides an excellent opportunity for Americans of all races and ethnic backgrounds to learn about Mexico's history and enjoy her culture and traditions.

Make a Piñata

You will need:

- ✔ balloon
- ✔ newspaper
- ✔ flour
- ✔ bowl
- ✔ water
- ✔ masking tape

- ✔ colored tissue paper
- ✔ poster paint
- ✔ paintbrush
- ✔ glue
- ✔ scissors

- ✔ yarn
- ✔ small wrapped candies
- ✔ plastic baseball bat
- ✔ scarf or blindfold

What to Do:

1. Blow up the balloon and tie tightly.

2. Tear a newspaper into strips about 1 inch wide and 12 inches long.

3. In a bowl, mix 5 cups of flour with water. Add the water slowly until the mixture is like pancake batter.

4. Dip the newspaper strips in the mixture until they are completely wet. Wipe off extra water with your fingers.

5. Drape the wet newspaper strips over the balloon. Overlap them until the balloon is completely covered. Continue adding newspaper until the balloon is covered with five to ten layers.

6. Let your piñata dry completely. (This may take a day or two.) To make an animal shape, use toilet tissue rolls and other cardboard. Use masking tape to hold the pieces on. What animal shapes can you make?

7 Decorate your piñata by painting it and gluing on bits of colored tissue paper.

8 To fill the piñata, cut a small flap in the top and bend it back. Pour in small wrapped candies. Then fold the flap closed.

9 Ask an adult to help you. Use a piece of yarn to hang the piñata from a doorway or tree branch. Then blind-fold each player and have him or her try to smash the piñata with the plastic baseball bat. Have players take turns until the piñata breaks and everyone can share the candy!

GLOSSARY

annexed—Controlled and incorporated by another country.

asylum—Protection given by a country to people escaping from another country.

bankrupt—Not having enough money to pay debts.

bilingual—Able to speak two languages.

boycott—Refusing to buy something or take part in something as a protest.

cavalry—Soldiers mounted on horseback.

charro (CHA-ro)—A traditional outfit worn by Mexican men during Cinco de Mayo.

China Poblana (CHEEN-ah poh-BLAH-nah)—A traditional outfit worn by Mexican women during Cinco de Mayo.

conservative—Someone who likes things to stay as they are; traditional.

constitution—The system of laws in a country.

criollos (cree-OH-yohs)—People of Spanish descent who were born in Mexico.

customs—Payments to a country from those entering from other nations.

dictator—Someone who has complete control of a country.

diplomats—People who represent their government in a foreign country.

executed—Killed by the government as punishment for committing a crime.

exiled—Sent to another country to live.

folklorico (fohk-LORE-ih-koh)—Traditional Mexican dancing.

indigenous—People who are native to a country.

jarabe tapatio (hah-RAH-bay tah-PAH-tee-oh)—A traditional Mexican dance; also called the Mexican hat dance.

liberal—In favor of political reform and progress.

mariachi (mah-ree-AH-chee)—Traditional Mexican music, featuring a fast, lively beat.

mole poblano (moh-LAY poh-BLAH-noh)—A traditional Mexican meal of a spicy sauce served over chicken or turkey and red rice.

radical—Believing in extreme political change.

rebellions—Armed fights against the government.

zapateado (zah-pah-tay-AH-doh)—A type of Mexican dancing where dancers pound their heels into floor.

CHAPTER NOTES

Chapter 1. Attack!

1. "The Battle of Pueblo and Cinco de Mayo," *The Border*, n.d., <http://www.pbs.org/kpbs/theborder/history/timeline/10.html> (August 22, 2005).
2. Ibid.
3. Ibid.
4. Ibid.

Chapter 2. The History of Cinco de Mayo

1. "Cortes, Hernan," *Microsoft Encarta 2000* CD-ROM.
2. "Mexico: Independence," *Microsoft Encarta 2000* CD-ROM.
3. "Manifest Destiny: An Introduction," *The Border*, n.d., <http://www.pbs.org/kera/us mexicanwar/dialogues/prelude/manifest/> (August 22, 2005).
4. "Mexico: Independence."
5. "Mexican-American War," *Wikipedia*, n.d., http://en.wikipedia.org/wiki/Mexican_American_War> (August 22, 2005).

6. "The Treaty of Guadalupe," *Library of Congress Hispanic Reading Room,* n.d., <http://www.loc.gov/rr/hispanic/ghtreaty/> (February 15, 2006).

7. "Treaty of Guadalupe," *Wikipedia,* n.d., <http://en.wikipedia.org/w/index.php?title =Treaty_of_Guadalupe> (February 15, 2006).

8. "Mexico: Independence."

9. "Mexican Holidays: Cinco de Mayo," n.d., <http://www.mexonline.com/cinco.htm> (August 22, 2005).

10. "Benito Juárez" *Dictionary of Hispanic Biography Gale Research,* 1996, <http://galenet.galegroup.com/servlet/BioRC> (August 22, 2005).

11. Ibid.

12. "History of the Zapotecs," *Indigenous People,* n.d., <http://www.indigenouspeople.net/Zapotec.htm> (February 15, 2006).

13. Ibid.

14. Ibid.

15. "Benito Juarez."

16. "The Battle of Pueblo and Cinco de Mayo," *The Border,* n.d., <http://www.pbs.org/kpbs/theborder/history/timeline/10.html> (August 22, 2005).

17. "Antonio Lopez de Santa Anna," *PBS.org,* n.d., <http://www.pbs.org/weta/thewest/

people/s_z/santaanna.htm> (February 15, 2006).

18. Ibid.

19. "Napoleon III," *Microsoft Encarta 2000* CD-ROM.

20. "Mexican Holidays: Cinco de Mayo."

21. "Cinco de Mayo de 1862—La Batalla de Puebla," n.d., <http://www.nacnet.org/ assunta/spa5may.htm> (August 22, 2005).

22. "Celebrate! Holidays in the U.S.A.: Cinco de Mayo," n.d., <http://www.usemb.se/ Holidays/celebrate/cincode.html> (August 22, 2005).

23. "General Ignacio Zaragoza," *Presidio La Bahia,* n.d., <http://www.presidiolabahia. org/zaragoza.htm> (February 15, 2006).

24. "Cinco de Mayo de 1862—La Batalla de Puebla."

25. Ibid.

26. Valerie Menard, *The Latino Holiday Book: From Cinco de Mayo to Dia de los Muertos— The Celebrations and Traditions of Hispanic-Americans,* updated and expanded second edition (New York: Marlowe and Company, 2004), p. 31.

27. "Celebrate! Holidays in the U.S.A.: Cinco de Mayo."

28. "Maximilian," *Microsoft Encarta 2000* CD-ROM.

29. Kevin Turner, "Maximilian Biography," n.d., <http://staff.esuhsd.org/~balochie/studentprojects/maximilian/> (August 22, 2005).

30. "Civil War Summary," *Civil War*, n.d., <http://www.civil-war.ws/summary> (February 15, 2006).

31. "Celebrate! Holidays in the U.S.A.: Cinco de Mayo."

32. Menard, p. 33.

Chapter 3. **Cultural Significance of Cinco de Mayo**

1. "Cinco de Mayo: A Symbol for Right of Nations to Self-Determination," *Houston Chronicle*, May 3, 1996.

2. Valerie Menard, *The Latino Holiday Book: From Cinco de Mayo to Dia de los Muertos—The Celebrations and Traditions of Hispanic-Americans*, updated and expanded second edition (New York: Marlowe and Company, 2004), p. 33.

3. Laurie Kay Sommers, "Symbol and Style in Cinco de Mayo." *Journal of American Folklore*, volume 98, 1995, p. 86.

4. Menard, p. 34.

5. "The Civil Rights Movement," *CNN*, n.d., <http://www.cnn.com/EVENST/1997/mlk/links.html> (February 15, 2006).

6. Sommers, p. 86.

7. "Lesson Plan: Mexican Independence Day," *Teacherlink*, n.d., <http://teacherlink.ed.usu.edu/Hresources/units/Byrnes-celebrations/> (February 15, 2006).

8. "Cinco de Mayo," *Wikipedia*, n.d., <http://en.wikipedia.org/wiki/Cinco_de_mayo> (August 22, 2005).

9. Ibid.

10. Ibid.

11. Richard L. Vazquez, "Cinco de Mayo," May 20, 2001, <http://www.lasculturas.com/content/view/ee/9/> (August 22, 2005).

12. "Bilingual Education Act of 1968," n.d., <http://si.unm.edu/ttwesol/timeline%20final/timeline2.html> (August 22, 2005).

13. Ibid.

14. Ibid.

15. Ibid.

16. Rodolfo F. Acuna. *Anything but Mexican: Chicanos in Contemporary Los Angeles*. New York: Verso, 1995, p. 36.

17. Ibid., p. 36.

18. Ibid., p. 38.

19. Richard L. Vazquez, "Cinco de Mayo," May 20, 2001, <http://www.lasculturas.com/content/view/ee/9/> (August 22, 2005).

20. Ibid.

21. Ibid.

22. Julia Layton, "Cinco de Mayo—What Does It Celebrate?", n.d., <http://www.banderas news.com/0504/nr-cincodemayo.htm> (August 22, 2005).

Chapter 4. Who Celebrates Cinco de Mayo?

1. "Mexican Holidays: Cinco de Mayo," n.d., <http://www.mexonline.com/cinco.htm> (August 22, 2005).

2. May Herz, "Cinco de Mayo," n.d., <http://www.inside-mexico.com/featurecinco.htm> (August 22, 2005).

3. Ibid.

4. Julia Layton, "Cinco de Mayo—What Does It Celebrate?", n.d., <http://www.banderas news.com/0504/nr-cincodemayo.htm> (August 22, 2005).

5. May Herz.

6. Julia Layton.

7. "Mexican Holidays: Cinco de Mayo."

8. Ibid.

9. Sandra Hernandez, "Cinco de Mayo, Once a Mexican Militia Victory, Now an Excuse to Party in U.S.," *Florida Sun Sentinel*, May 5, 2005.
10. Ibid.
11. Ibid.
12. Ibid.

◈ Chapter 5. Symbols of Cinco de Mayo

1. Robert Bryce, "Forget the Macarena: Texas High Schools Do the Mariachi." *Christian Science Monitor*, volume 88, October 9, 1996, p. 3.
2. "History of the Mariachi: Excerpts from *Mexico, The Meeting of Two Cultures*, New York: Higgins and Associates, 1991," n.d., <http://www.mariachi.org/history.html> (August 22, 2005).
3. Ibid.
4. Ibid.
5. Bryce, p. 3.
6. Zsofia Budai, "Ballet Folklorico Gets On Its Toes," April 4, 2003, <http://www.thehoya.com/guide/040403/guide2.cfm> (August 22, 2005).
7. Ibid.
8. Ibid.

9. "History of the Mariachi: Excerpts from *Mexico, The Meeting of Two Cultures,* New York: Higgins and Associates, 1991."
10. "The Mexican Hat Dance," n.d. <http://www. mexfoldanco.org/jarabe.htm> (August 22, 2005).
11. Zsofia Budai.
12. "The Mexican Hat Dance."
13. "Mexico: Independence," *Microsoft Encarta 2000* CD-ROM.
14. Ibid.
15. Ibid.
16. Ibid.
17. Ibid.
18. "History of the Mariachi: Excerpts from *Mexico, The Meeting of Two Cultures,* New York: Higgins and Associates, 1991."
19. Darlene Gallardo "What My Culture Means to Me," *Hispanic,* volume 8, March 1995, p. 92.
20. "The Mexican Hat Dance."
21. Julia Layton, "Cinco de Mayo—What Does It Celebrate?", n.d., <http://www.banderas news.com/0504/nr-cincodemayo.htm> (August 22, 2005).

Chapter 6. Cinco de Mayo Today

1. Julia Layton, "Cinco de Mayo—What Does It Celebrate?", n.d., <http://www.banderas

news.com/0504/nr-cincodemayo.htm>
(August 22, 2005).

2. "Men's Costumes—Cinco de Mayo," n.d.,
<http://www.hpl.lib.tx.us/youth/cinco_
men.html> (August 22, 2005).

3. Ibid.

4. "Women's Costumes—Cinco de Mayo," n.d.,
<http://www.hpl.lib.tx.us/youth/cinco_
women.html> (August 22, 2005).

5. May Herz, "Cinco de Mayo," n.d., <http://
www.inside-mexico.com/featurecinco.htm>
(August 22, 2005).

6. Julia Layton.

7. Valerie Menard, *The Latino Holiday Book:
From Cinco de Mayo to Dia de los Muertos—
The Celebrations and Traditions of Hispanic-
Americans*, updated and expanded second
edition (New York: Marlowe and Company,
2004), p. 37.

8. "Celebrate! Holidays in the U.S.A.: Cinco
de Mayo," n.d., <http://www.usemb.se/
Holidays/celebrate/cincode.html> (August
22, 2005).

9. Menard, pp. 36–37.

10. Menard, p. 37.

11. "About Viva! Cinco de Mayo," April 24, 2004,
<http://www.vivacincodemayo.org/about.
htm> (August 22, 2005).

12. "Celebrate Culture," n.d., <http://www.newsed.org/new/culturebody.htm#cinco> (August 22, 2005).

13. Ibid.

14. "Cinco de Mayo Fiesta," n.d., <http://www.fiestacincodemayo.com> (August 22, 2005).

15. Ana Ledo, "Cinco de Mayo Celebration a First for New York," *El Diariolla Prensa*, April 12, 2002.

16. Menard, p. 38.

FURTHER READING

Alter, Judy. *Mexican Americans.* Chanhassen, Minn.: Child's World, 2003.

Calvert, Patricia. *Hernando Cortés: Fortune Favored the Bold.* New York: Benchmark Books, 2003.

García, Aurora Colón. *Cinco de Mayo.* Chicago, Ill.: Heinemann Library, 2003.

Hodgkins, Fran. *Mexico: A Question and Answer Book.* Mankato, Minn.: Capstone Press, 2005.

Hunter, Amy N. *The History of Mexico.* Philadelphia, Penn.: Mason Crest Publishers, 2003.

Nobleman, Marc Tyler. *Cinco de Mayo.* Minneapolis, Minn.: Compass Point Books, 2005.

Peppas, Lynn. *Life in Ancient Mesoamerica.* New York: Crabtree Pub. Co., 2005.

Sanna, Ellyn. *Mexican Americans' Role in the United States: A History of Pride, A Future of Hope.* Philadelphia, Penn.: Mason Crest Publishers, 2006.

Turck, Mary C. *Mexico and Central America: A Fiesta of Culture, Crafts, and Activities for Ages 8-12.* Chicago, Ill.: Chicago Review Press, 2004.

INTERNET ADDRESSES

Holiday Fun: Cinco de Mayo Celebration

<http://www.kidsdomain.com/holiday/cinco/>

Click on different links to read about the history of Cinco de Mayo, and find some crafts and e-cards.

México for Kids

<http://www.elbalero.gob.mx/index_kids.html>

Learn more about Mexico from this Web site.

INDEX